Meditation
for Kids
(and other beings)

Laurie Fisher Huck

WEATHERHILL
New York • Tokyo

© 1995 by Laurie Fisher Huck

First Weatherhill edition, 1996

Published by Weatherhill, Inc., of New York and Tokyo, with editorial offices at 568 Broadway, Suite 705, New York, N.Y. 10012. Protected by copyright under the terms of the International Copyright Union; all rights reserved. First published by Red Dory Press. Printed in the United States.

Library of Congress Cataloging-in-Publication Data

Huck, Laurie Fisher.
    Meditation for kids (and other beings) / Laurie Fisher Huck. —
1st Weatherhill ed.
        p.   cm.
    Originally published: Lunenburg, Canada: Red Dory Press, 1993.
    Summary: Illustrations and simple text describe the what and how of meditation.
    ISBN 0-8348-0355-0 (pbk.)
    1. Meditation—Psychological aspects—Juvenile literature.
I. Title
BF637.M4H83 1996

158'.12—dc20
95-52078

CIP
AC

To _anyone_ brave enough to sit still
for more than ~~twenty~~ minutes.
        TEN

editation
means
different
things
to
different
people.

Now
you have
a very
clear idea
of what
meditation
is...

...not!

The
point
is..

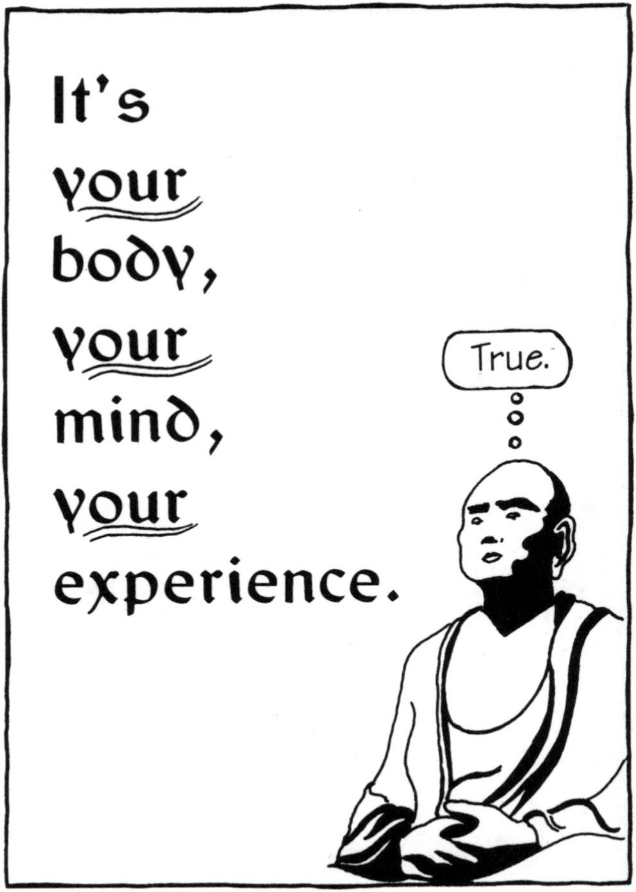
It's your body, your mind, your experience.
True.

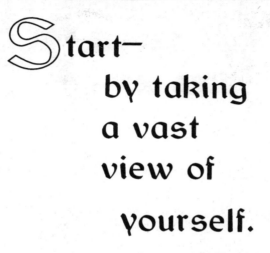

Start—
by taking
a vast
view of
yourself.

Basically,
you
are
a
kind,
intelligent
human
being.

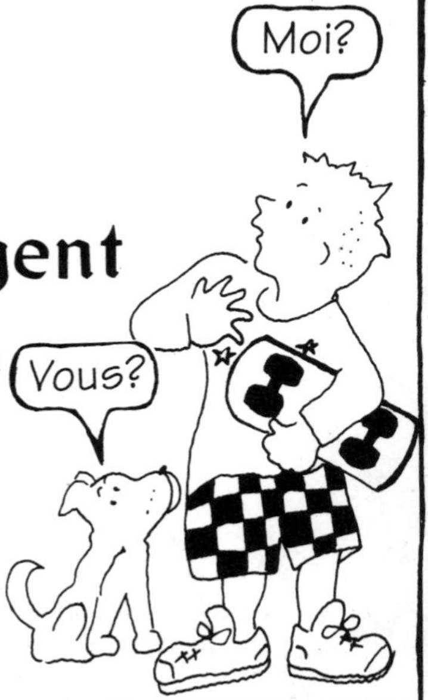

You
can
become
wise...

and of
benefit
to this
planet.

Meditation

is a tool

that can
help make
these
wishes

come
true.

If you are:

☐ The popular, super cool type
or

☐ The cheerful, likeable type
or

☐ The quiet type
or

☐ The visitor from planet X type
or

☐ The bossy pants type
or

☐ The basketball player type
or

☐ The save the planet type
or

☐ The confused and unhappy type
or

☐ The baseball card dealer type
or

☐ The love to have fun type
or

☐ The loner type

or

☐ The "I wanna run away" type

or

☐ The gorgeous, too cool to live type

or

☐ The weirdo type

or

☐ The neanderthal type

or

☐ The know all the dinosaurs type

or

☐ The good at everything type

or

☐ The hidden genius type

or

☐ The jog before breakfast type

or

☐ The artistic type

or

☐ The I want to make a difference type

or

☐ The wear only the best gear type
    or
☐ The hair obsessed type
    or
☐ The can't stop talking type
    or
☐ The discipline problem type
    or
☐ The "give me a break" type
    or
☐ The gotta watch TV type
    or
☐ The 50,000 ideas at once type
    or
☐ The play the piano *and* violin type
    or
☐ The "Archie" comic book type
    or
☐ The glued to a computer type
    or
☐ The everyone else is weird type
    or

☐ The always listening to music type

or

☐ The moody type

or

☐ The grumpy type

or

☐ The star athlete type

or

☐ The world is going to pieces type

or

☐ The do things for others type

or

☐ The travel alot type

or

☐ The have no money type

or

☐ The read this whole list type

or

☐ ALL OF THE ABOVE (depending on day, year, allowance, and latest haircut)

Then you might
really enjoy
discovering
what
meditation
can
be
for
you.

Sometimes: wild...

...fun...

...peaceful...

Most
of what
happens
in your
life...

starts
in the
ocean
of
your mind.

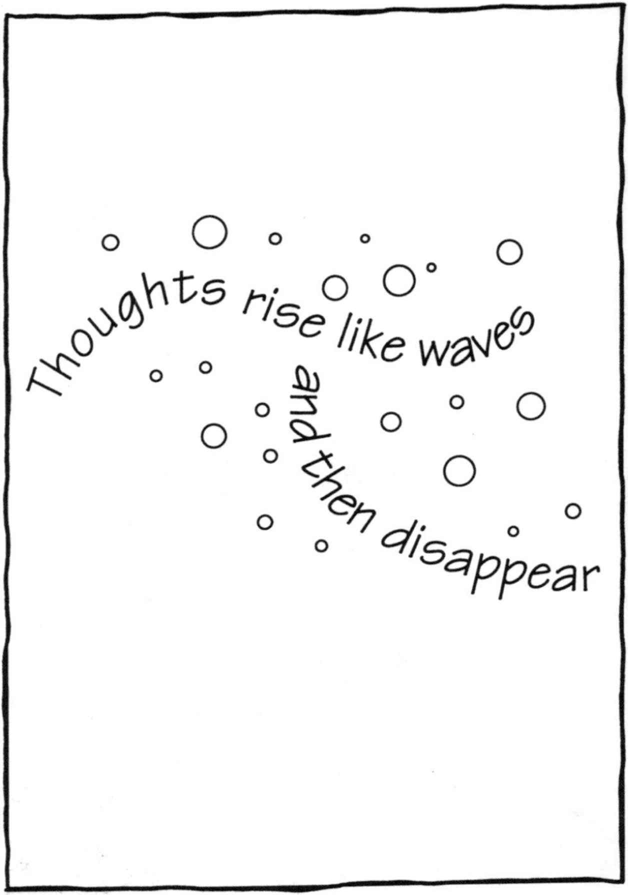
Thoughts rise like waves
and then disappear

Practicing meditation
is like great scuba-gear:

You can see, hear, touch,
and taste your thoughts
without drowning in them.

Your
mind
is
like
a

horse...

beautiful,
independant,
and
strong.

Being a
good rider
takes
practice

Come Back

There are

are

two

things

you

should

know.

You
have a
mind.

It
thinks.
(a lot!)

When
you
meditate
you
sit
still

and let your mind relax...

As
your
mind
relaxes...

your thoughts start to settle.

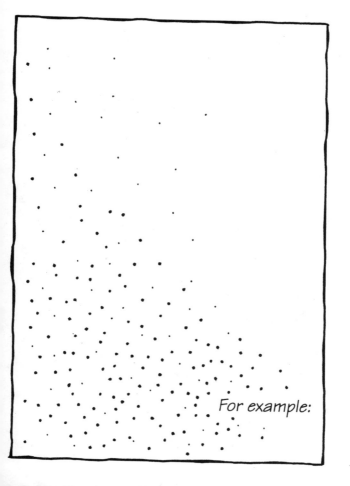

For example:

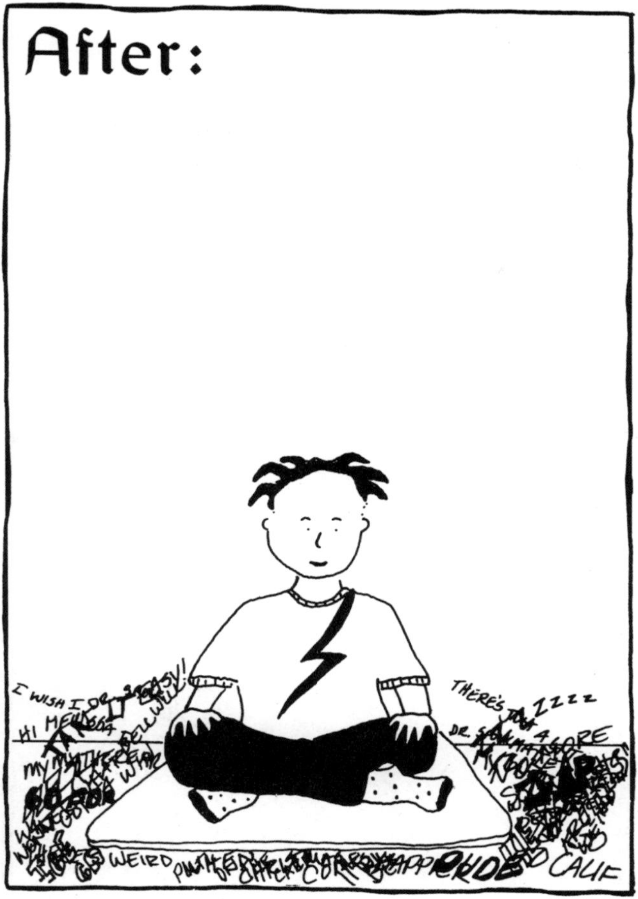
After:
WEIRD
CALIF

By
not making
a
BIG
DEAL
out of
any
thought.

and come back to
your breath.

sitting
breathing
sitting
*...Boy, a peanutbutter
sandwich would sure taste
good. Maybe I'll...*
"Thinking"
sitting
breathing
sitting
breathing
sitting
breathing
*...Oh yeah. I can't believe
Marlys said that about
me...*
"Thinking"
sitting
...I"ll kill her
"Thinking"
breathing
sitting
...With a gun
"Thinking"

...Better yet, a machete!
"Thinking"
>sitting
>breathing
>sitting

...It's quiet in here
"Thinking"
>breathing
>sitting
>breathing
>sitting

...YIKES!! I didn't get my money from Mrs. Row and...
"Thinking"
>breathing
>sitting

...WHEW!! That must be what...
"Thinking"
>breathing
>sitting
>breathing
>sitting

...My butt hurts.
>ad nauseum...

Boring?

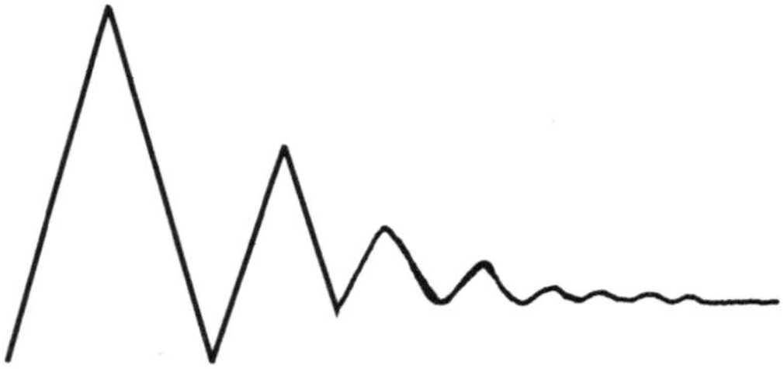

Yes, but...

real.

The funny
thing about
meditation is:
you start
wanting
to
do it.

Maybe
you begin
to notice
that
coming back
feels better
than
not
coming back.

When you are:

happy
confused
angry
sad
excited
thrilled
fuzzy-minded
brilliant
lost
irritated
nervous
spooked
confident
unsure
guilty
delighted
just plain weird

 *whatever...*

Just
sit.

Come
back
to
where
you
are.

There's
no
place
like
it.

A Note from the Author

If you feel inspired to meditate, it is important to have a real, live, flesh and blood teacher, someone you can trust and someone who has a lot of meditation experience. If you don't know anyone, write to me at P.O. Box 538, Lunenburg, Nova Scotia BOJ 2CO, and I will help you in any way I can.

Laurie Fisher Huck

Picture of the author

Before 10 years of meditation.

After 10 years of meditation.